Minimalism

With This Insightful Guide, You Will Learn How Adopting A Minimalist Lifestyle Can Not Only Improve Your Health But Also Increase Your Income And Bring You Greater Happiness

Denis Baier

TABLE OF CONTNET

Subterranean Spaces: 1

How Living Minimally Lowers Stress 12

Abilitation Into A Simple Life 23

Substance Minimalism Is International. 37

Sustaining Minimalism: Some Advice 53

Assists You In Improving The World 65

Time Management 78

Comprehending The Mindset Of Minimalism 88

Internal, Not External, Is Minimalism. 104

Putting The Organisation Process In Motion 116

Establish A Precise Intention, Deadline, And Goal. 136

Subterranean Spaces:

Store larger quantities or infrequently occurring items that could not fit in your home's main rooms can be kept in basements. Clothes offices to a house are housed in multiple cellars. Keep in mind that many cellars may be damp. Unless you have a finished storm cellar with climate control, they will almost certainly be colder and damper if they are not wet. Make the most of this information to your advantage, and consider carefully what you store in a storm cellar. Examine the items in your storm cellar and the reasons for their placement. While some items, especially those that are only infrequently used, seem appropriate to store in a storm cellar, others are just junk you will never use again.

Attic:

Basements and attics are similar, except that attics are typically located on higher floors of your house. Many lofts are quite close areas that allow for some storage but may not be available. Avoid developing the habit of throwing stuff in your storage area to deal with at a later time. The attic can be a terrific spot to store items you are positive you will use later on—if not now, then definitely soon—and keep them out of sight.

Garage: The primary purpose of a carport is—or rather it should be—to house your cars so that they are protected from the elements outside.

Unfortunately, many people use their carports as places to keep unnecessary items and clutter rather than their automobiles, which are more expensive to secure. First, try to turn the carport into a home for your cars. Nothing you don't think is amazing or precious should be allowed inside your carport.

Closets: Closets are distinct spaces where items may accumulate due to external factors. Assign each wardrobe to particular items or collections of items. For instance, one wardrobe might have winter coats, sweaters, and shoes. Decide how many items you need, then throw away the rest. Make the necessary adjustments so that everything in your clothing is readily available. Something must be removed if it does not fit inside.

Simplifying Throughout The Whole Home

Your entire home can be minimalist if that's what you want. These days, many homes are built to offer the highest level of productivity at an amazing value. These homes have hardly enough square footage to be functional and comfortable, fewer rooms than you'll need, and more basic rooms that barely meet the necessities. The reserve money accumulates when you have a smaller area to heat or cool. You probably don't have many items you can plug into outlets if you live a minimalist lifestyle. This adds up to a whopping financial expenditure in power.

These smaller homes save even more time for cleaning and organizing, which is a benefit most people value. People may think living in such little confines is absurd, but they will still laugh all the way to the bank. Although having a home like this made specifically could seem expensive, keep in mind that, if done well, the cost of supplies should be significantly lower with a more modest and well-functioning home. This could also mean "minimizing" to a house that better meets your needs. With kids and other people living in your house, you might no longer need what you formerly or believed you desired.

So how will you handle everything that you have removed from your home and will never be a part of your moderate lifestyle again? You may start by taking anything of considerable value and offering it for sale online or through a yard sale. Most items will be taken from you by Noble Cause, and those who organize your deductions will typically receive a desk job to a duty allowance at the end of the year. You could trade items for something you value more. Various items essentially belong to the recyclable or rubbish categories. Organizing everything from start to finish could save you a significant amount of money, especially if you have many possessions you want to take with you.

Reducing: The Assembling Event

Many minimalists have decided to hold their own "pressing party" to determine what exactly is essential. Bringing everything in your house together is what this celebration is all about. Items that fit into boxes are grouped along with the spaces they would typically occupy and placed inside them. You might throw a sheet or another cover over larger items that aren't necessarily packaged. Choose a time frame that works for you, and tell yourself that it's not important to you if you haven't released anything after three weeks.

Of course, essentials like your refrigerator and its contents will immediately become important. Your bed, toothbrush, oven, and other necessities will shortly be quickly unpacked. Throughout the long term, carefully consider what is crazy and far away from you. Don't unload anything just to keep them around. When your mind consciously considers something and informs you that you should or might want to use it, you might be able to release some of the tension associated with it.

If you decide to hold a pressing party, enjoy yourself immensely. Think of it as a chance to start over with your resources, now realizing what is most important to you. When the predetermined amount of time has passed, decide whether to donate the items to a worthy cause or sell them to generate additional revenue.

Reducing Using a Predetermined Amount of Items:

Some minimalists, the most dedicated among them, decide to live with a certain number of possessions or close to that number. These minimalists usually choose to have 100 items. These people then use this benchmark and carry their quantity of assets to go closer to their goal. The figure encompasses all items claimed, including bed linens, flatware, toothbrushes, clothes, etc.

A great alternative idea is that maintaining a reasonable lifestyle replenishes your energy reserves. Some people take it as a reminder that there are things we give up in our homes when they enter their homes and see the disarray around them. The disarray may remind us that we always fall behind on tasks or focus too much on one area of our lives while ignoring another. Furthermore, assets possess an extraordinary power over us: they firmly install us in areas where we are not required to be. Because we would prefer not to handle the chaos of messiness inside our houses, having too many assets might almost make it seem like a task to go after that new position and move to that other state to take it.

We, therefore, use our messiness and possessions as an excuse for not being able to accept the job offer that would undoubtedly make us happier at the moment, even though it pays marginally less.

Given that your possessions are "breaking you down," how much life are you missing out on?

When you have less of them, you are better equipped to overcome those obstacles and relocate, explore, and visit places that might ultimately lead to your pleasure.

Nevertheless, letting go of the "examination game" is one of the best possible benefits of maintaining a balanced lifestyle. The items we own mark our abundance, self-worth, and financial well-being in the eyes of the broader public. Children are positioned in the center of school based on what they wear, whether or not it is a name brand. Kids are positioned in a secondary school based on the kind of gear they carry around, even whether it's the newest iPhone model. The connection and positioning game remains the same in the adult world.

How Living Minimally Lowers Stress

Many financial burdens contribute to a significant reduction in stress. The primary cause of unease, whether alone or with others, is financial problems and stress. Cash and finances put a strain on people, so being able to reduce and put more money back in your pocket is helpful.

However, that isn't the primary reason maintaining a modest and uncomplicated lifestyle helps relieve stress and anxiety.

Our perspective is always changing due to visual changes. This explains why "shading impact" is one of the most well-known topics in brain research. Colors elicit explicit emotions because of the lessons we learn as children and how they are ingrained in our fundamental knowledge and neural pathways. Because so many other, more complex kinds of information are influenced by the associations we formed as children, many people associate blue with "relief" and red with "outrage."

This is also the foundational idea of acknowledgment—the potential for a visual enhancement to aid someone in revisiting an event, memory, or emotional response. However, this labor never stops being done. Whenever you take in something outside, the things surrounding you elicit positive and genuine feelings, and filling your life with meaningless things might make someone feel trapped and insane. The visual upgrade progresses from a constrained experience to an open sensation by removing those items and creating more liberated and wide areas, which can play tricks on the mind and cause a more relaxed response.

However, maintaining a balanced style of living means you won't ever again need to be conscious of trends. By escaping a pointless everyday living centeredaround name-brand products and always innovative advancements, you break free from the constraints of "must have to be commendable." Your possessions do not typify your identity. We ultimately become completely wrapped in the same thing: ourselves. If your possessions are how you define yourself, you will always feel like you must spend all the money you may have to feel good enough. This feeling might cause you to become perpetually restless, characterized by frailty, carelessness, and seriousness.

Benefits of Minimalism, Chapter 2.

A minimalist lifestyle stresses that "simple is better" concerning one's surroundings, possessions, attitude, or other areas of life.

You can live a simpler and more liberated existence by clearing your life of all clutter by adopting a minimalist lifestyle. Living a minimalist lifestyle has several benefits, including time and financial savings.

Eliminating clutter is the first step towards living a minimalist lifestyle. It can include decluttering your house, setting up your workspace, or closely examining your beliefs.

Since you can live lightly in every area of your life, there are no official minimalist guidelines. Whichever minimalist strategy you decide on, start by decluttering and planning your lifestyle from the perspective of "less is more."

Numerous benefits of minimalism could make you feel more invigorated and in control of your life.

You should consider minimalism to see if it can assist you in reducing the reasons for your feelings of preoccupation, confusion, or disturbance. Even if you're content with your circumstances, you might still benefit from simplifying your life.

Reducing clutter is a guaranteed way to boost your productivity.

You'll probably notice some good advantages in your life almost immediately after you embark on your minimalist journey. The benefits can vary greatly and last longer, depending on your preferred minimalist lifestyle.

1. CREATE MORE ROOM:

Because they have fewer items to store, minimalists typically have large closets in their apartments.

While having fewer things is usually the aim of becoming a minimalist, having extra storage space could help keep certain essentials.

2. SAVE MONEY ON HOUSE FURNISHINGS: Keeping up with house décor can result in major financial savings. The costs of furniture can quickly mount up.

Investing in key décor pieces that make sense for you and your style might help you embrace the "few is better" philosophy.

3. VALUING YOUR BELONGINGS MORE: Having a lot of possessions might make it easier to overlook the true worth of each one. If you own less, you might find that you are more appreciative of what you have and take better care of your belongings.

4. FOCUS ON WHAT COUNTS: Material belongings are less important than memories. Therefore, if you spend less time focused on your possessions, you'll have more opportunities to be present in the future moments that will matter most to you.

5. ADOPT AND SATISFY A CLUTTER-FREE attitude: Having a clutter-free attitude may have a positive impact on a variety of areas of your life, including your home, workplace, car, and even how you arrange your thoughts.

6. FINDING YOUR POSSESSIONS QUICKLY: It can be quite annoying to look for a misplaced item at home, but having fewer possessions lowers your likelihood of going through this ordeal. Maintaining constant inventory control is much simpler when you live a minimalist lifestyle.

7. MAKE MONEY FROM UNWANTED ITEMS: Giving away items you no longer need is one of the first steps towards being a minimalist. A quick and easy way

to increase your income is to sell the items you no longer need.

8. SPEND LESS TIME AND ENERGY CLEANING: You'll need more time and energy to clean the more items you own. On average, it can take up to six hours to clean your house, which you would much rather spend doing something else.

9. WORKING WITH MINIMAL OR NO DISTRACTIONS: By minimizing visible distractions, a minimal workstation or workspace will support your ability to remain focused and committed.

Eliminating non-work-related items, desk toys, electronics, and materials will help you begin your workday with a clean head.

10. MAKING TRAVEL PREPARATION EASY: Minimalism makes travel easier for those who enjoy it since it reduces the amount of stuff they need to bring, which saves time and money.

11. BREATHE HEALTHIER: A cleaner, healthier atmosphere results from having fewer possessions in your home, which also means less dust, dirt, and toxins.

A minimalist home typically has a fresher scent because there are fewer sources of pollution there.

12. IMPROVE YOUR MENTAL WELLBEING: A messy, disorganized home can harm our general mental wellbeing because we reflect our environment. A straightforward, tidy

environment may reduce stress and despair while promoting mental focus.

AbilitationInto A Simple Life

You ought to lead a simple life. The absence of complexity, hardship, or effort, or the presence of luxury, pretense, or ritual, is what simplicity is free from.

What can you quantify?

Is it a larger home that will take more time and money to maintain?

Is it the new stuff that the fashion industry is embracing?

How much of what you own is truly necessary?

Examine everything in each room critically as you move through them. Is it an asset or a liability? How much of the cutter do you not even get to "see" anymore? What can you get rid of? If something doesn't serve a purpose or appeal to you, eliminate it. Sell it. Give it a shot. Take it.

Analyze your obligations carefully. How worthwhile are the things you devote your time to? Are you aware that you have 3600 seconds every day? What value do you derive from your investment of time, money, and resources?

Embrace yourself:

Is this a significant activity?

What does it mean to me?

Does it have top priority?

Does it advance my personal growth?

If not, remove yourself from the commitment. Rethink and redraw your calendar and schedule. Learn to say no without apology or remorse.

You must put an end to your media binge. You could be doing more useful things with the time you spend watching TV, responding to emails, and browsing the internet. One of the simplest ways to simplify your life is to stop consuming so much information, especially negative information like the news that floods your mind.

Crucial for Practice If You Desire to Lead a Simple Life with Accurate Self-Knowledge

Understanding who you are will help you on this journey. You must identify the kind of minimalism to whom you belong. This is the place to start, always. We cannot make choices that will lead to a more fulfilling and whole existence unless we have a clear grasp of our values, motives, and preferences.

Eliminate the extra

Accept the need to say "No":

Every decision is a trade-off between qualities and timing; the more you add to your schedule and responsibilities, the more trade-offs you will have to make." Projects, commitments, and responsibilities: why must you perform every task like Andrew? In what direction do you draw the line between quantity and quality? Never forget that you have a choice.

An emphasis on non-impulsive consumption:

What is the reason behind your purchase decision? Does this product reflect your values? Too often, we don't even think before we buy. We respond with impulse."Living a simpler life might be a difficult task. Challenging physical and mental intricacies reveal the actual person beneath the surface. You will be concerned that you lack the necessary drive, intelligence, toughness, or uniqueness to possibly lead a simple life. When the real phenomenon is exposed and there is no longer any need to pretend, exceptions cease to exist."

Advice for Lead a More Simplified Life

Are you sick and weary of leading an idle life and want to know how to lead a simple existence? If so, you should read these strategies. These strategies will also boost your productivity.

Establish a daily routine.

Form constructive habits

Assign tasks to other individuals.

Get rid of anything unnecessary.

Create a to-do list.

Take some time to engage in social media.

Increase the amount of time spent with friends and family.

Why Live a Minimal Life?

My favorite benefit of being minimalist is that it makes cleaning much easier. This is one of the finest reasons to go minimalist. You see, it would be an understatement to say that I detest doing housekeeping and cleaning the house. However, I used to be confused about this: I also detest a dirty and disorganized home. I understand that I can't have my cake and eat it too (clean my house to a minimum) (and keep my home tidy and orderly).

I could finally have my cake and eat it when I adopted a simple lifestyle! I had to clean the house less frequently since there was so much less junk. And the house still appeared neat and well-organized!

Less clutter means I can spend less time removing items from the counter, cabinets, and tabletops to vacuum or wipe them clean of dust. Reduced clutter also meant fewer items to maneuver about to vacuum the floor thoroughly. I don't waste time rearranging items to make room for them and then putting them back where they belong because I can just vacuum the floor immediately.

Significantly Reduced Stress

The amount of stress you can eliminate is another reason you should try minimalism. How? Anybody's life is made unnecessarily stressful by clutter, and clutter only increases with possessions. Because minimalism is all about having less stuff, there is also less mess. There could not even be any chances for clutter! And a life free of clutter also means a life free of stress.

One way clutter increases stress is that it can make it extremely difficult to discover vital items. Additionally, searching through mountains of clutter to find your car keys in a hurry may be stressful. Keeping things where they belong, remembering where you put them, and finding them become quite simple when you have little to no clutter. Clutter can also contribute to stress by making it difficult to unwind, concentrate, or do both. Have you ever attempted to work on a pressing report or assignment in a disorganized room? If so, you likely had difficulty focusing or inspiring yourself. And I'm sure it would be an extremely stressful experience if the deadline for that assignment or report was approaching soon.

Self-assurance to Host Visitors

Having little to no clutter might make you feel more at ease and confident while hosting guests in your home or workplace. Not only will this give you greater self-assurance, but you'll be able to host guests at home with much ease, knowing that your workstation or home is sufficiently clean and organized to avoid last-minute cleaning.

Capacity to Succeed

How may having less clutter contribute to your success? Well, by enhancing your ability to concentrate at work. You see when you live a minimalist lifestyle, your workspace will also be clutter-free, in addition to your house. Additionally, you accomplish two goals at once if you work from home!

Those who are shy and very sensitive will find that a clutter-free environment is especially beneficial for their productivity. This is because when it comes to concentrating and getting down to business, these people are pickier about noise and disorder. In a very congested workplace, they can easily become overwhelmed and stressed that they cannot perform as needed. Additionally, having a messy home might make it difficult for you to unwind and rest, making it difficult to refuel for work the following day.

Satisfaction

Few people aspire to the virtue of contentment. It's not strange to find most people in great discontent in today's materialistic world, bolstered by a highly discontent-centered business environment that uses mass and social media to make people buy more items and get even richer. These days, many retail establishments feed the delusion to naive customers that "I'll only be happy when I get this or that!" which leads to a very materialistic and unhappy society. It's an illusion because the exhilaration soon wears off after you achieve your deepest desires, and you find yourself craving more.

Finding true contentment in life might be simple when leading a basic lifestyle. Why? Living a minimalist lifestyle can demonstrate that, in contrast to what the largest retailers of today try to convince us through the media and mass media, you can have the happiest possible life without owning a lot more stuff than you need. Once you realize that you only need one or a few of the newest iPhones, gadgets, outfits, and automobiles to get by, you'll quit chasing after them. You'll also realize that none of the previous excesses gave you much incremental delight and fulfillment. You'll be able to see for yourself that, when it comes to living a high-quality life, less really is more when you purge your life of unnecessary items.

DUPLICITY-FREEDOM IS MINIMALISM.

Even though most people don't realize it, they live in duplicity. They have three different lives: one focused on their family, one centered on their coworkers, and one on their neighbors. Their chosen lifestyle necessitates projecting a specific external image based on their circumstances. They are discarded by most recent advertising campaigns or the conditions of their employers.

Conversely, a straightforward life is cohesive and consistent. It has taught me a completely transferrable lifestyle, regardless of the circumstances. The life on Friday evening is the same as on Sunday morning. Since it's Monday morning, it is consistent, dependable, and unchanging. It functions in every situation.

Substance Minimalism Is International.

Celebrities are idolized in our world. They are photographed for magazines, featured in radio interviews, and returned for television. Many people envy them and hold their lives up to the ideal standard. The media does not influence those who lead minimalist lifestyles in the same manner. They don't mesh with the consumer culture that politicians and businesses promote. Still, they have a charming and appealing existence.

While most people go after fame, glamour, and success, minimalism speaks to us in a quieter, more peaceful tone. It encourages us to take it slowly, eat less, but appreciate life more. And when we see someone leading a simplified life, we frequently realize that we have been chasing the wrong things for a long time.

These Are The Six Types of Minimalism. Which One Do You Think You Are?

In contemporary culture, minimalism has become so synonymous with meaninglessness that it no longer seems to have any real significance. "Minimalism" is bandied about a lot and is presented without enough context to be understood.

It turns out that there are numerous variations on how to apply the same abstract, basic foundation. I therefore wanted to try my hand at explaining them and providing context and imagery for the various ways in which a person might contribute to minimalism.

There is a recurring theme: Whatever your level of minimalism, it's a lifestyle focused on less.

Visual Minimalists

It's all about the optimal values for the aesthetic minimum. They don't necessarily possess lesions, but they have them on display. Their favoritecolor is white, which they use for everything from dinnerware to walls to linens. Easier to grasp, the aesthetic minimalist is all about the visuals: Enter the front door of their colorful apartment and notice the bare countertops, floors, and walls (maybe save one piece of abstract art in a slender frame laid gingerly on top of a shaker-style bench).

Signature Motion: discarding their mismatched hangers in favor of an expensive set of contemporary hangers.

They could adore a sophisticated print of a continuous line drawing.

If you struggle to like who you are, cut off the depressing friendships and begin engaging in activities that will help you learn to respect who you are. Start to like who you are and what you stand for. Positive role models teach you how to move forward without letting others hold you back, so it's acceptable if you need one. See how you feel after attempting a few of the following:

Make time for a close friend and call them just to check in without focusing on yourself.

Serve soup in a soup kitchen as a volunteer.

Contribute to the local animal shelter.

Without bragging, take constructive actions that uphold your values. It doesn't operate the same way if you do it with strings attached; only you need to know.

Donate to a senior neighbor without anticipating gratitude or ego boosts.

You don't have to show others that you do any of these things to feel better about yourself. These are things you ought to take care of yourself. Just say you are too busy when someone calls you and asks you to do them a favor for the nth time. Less is always more, and you can live as you see fit. Eliminating those who take advantage of you releases you and allows you to form caring and helpful friendships. You'll also discover that you have more time to spend with your family and may value them even more.

Chapter 2: Three Easy Steps for Beginners of Minimalism

The minimalist lifestyle may appear difficult initially, and for a good reason—not everyone is adaptable. It would take discipline to embrace change, including planning, attention to detail, and concentration.

It is advisable to approach the shift to minimalist gradually, which is why this chapter will walk you through the three stages of beginning minimalism:

Step 1: Pick a single area of your life.

At different times during the day, we all assume different personas. For example, we could be the loving parent who makes sure their children eat a nutritious breakfast before school; later in the day, we might be the motivated employee who aspires to receive a big promotion; and at night, we might be the family chef who prepares delectable homemade dinners.

Our lives consist of so many facets we can occasionally feel overtaken by them. Now that you have a list, you may choose which one to simplify. For instance, you may like to lead a better lifestyle, but managing your diet and exercise is so difficult that you often ignore it completely. However, you will become more concentrated and engaged in your exercise regimen if you incorporate minimalist living.

After selecting that element, you go to Step 2.

Step 2: Make an easy 30-day schedule

Psychologists claim that for an action to become ingrained, it must be repeated for at least 21 days. The minimalist lifestyle, which consists of a few basic routines, is equivalent to this idea. Your life will become much less complicated after you put the following advice into practice, even though it may seem confusing and at odds with a minimalist existence.

Before creating your plan, list the behaviors you want to develop in that specific area of your life. Referring to the fitness example, you can list routines like "eat a plateful of vegetables with every meal" and "exercise for 30 minutes a day." You can narrow down your list to three or five items if it grows too big by listing them in order of importance.

The next stage is to create the most straightforward action plan for each habit after you've made a list of them. For example, your action plan might be to "watch a 30-minute workout video on YouTube at home" if your goal is to develop the habit of "exercising for 30 minutes a day." As far as minimalistic living goes, this is perfect since you can work out without leaving your house. No more wasting time traveling or extra cash on drinks outside after your workout.

As you develop your minimalist action plan, push your imagination and ingenuity because it will help you establish the habits faster.

Step 3: Evaluate Your Development

Take periodic breaks during your 30-day plan to evaluate its effectiveness and how it works for you. You can spend as little as fifteen minutes at the end of each week reflecting on yourself. Now is the ideal moment for you to reflect on your action plan and identify any issues so that you can alter it to better meet your objectives.

These summarize the three fundamental actions you can do to begin living a minimalist lifestyle. Remember that you are not trying to become more minimalist than anyone else. Making errors is OK if you correct them and get back on track. Never forget that you can live simply and contentedly every day.

Next, proceed room by room and discard anything extra you can live without for the time being. If anything is too ingrained in your prior experiences for you to let go of, try not to freak out and put yourself through unnecessary stress. Many discover that it will take two or three iterations to fully eliminate everything cluttering their houses, even when decluttering room by room.

Decluttering can involve organizing items as well as getting rid of them. To have records available for everything crucial they interact with, including their cars, health care, medical bills, and critical documents, many people still use paperwork. Even while leading a minimalist lifestyle might be quite affordable, there are instances when you need to purchase to keep organized. Investing in a filing cabinet or hanging folders that fit into empty pull-out cabinets is a reasonably priced way to gather all those crucial documents strewn everywhere and keep them somewhere you can readily access.

Decluttering closets may prove to be the most difficult task for some individuals. Some people's wardrobes are naturally large, while others are naturally small. If your closet is naturally spacious, consider the following advice for organizing your clothes: Take out a bin, place it behind you, and start carefully removing each article of clothes one at a time. Throw it in the trash and throw it behind your head if you haven't worn it in a year. You can sell or donate these clothing items, and it will assist you in determining what you actually wear and what you just hang onto because you can.

Using number-based methods is another approach to simplify your house. You can go through your house as long as you need to, load up a garbage bag with items you no longer need, and then donate or discard them. Another option is to participate in the 12-12-12 Challenge, which involves going through your house and identifying 12 items you can give, 12 items you can discard, and 12 items that can be put back in their rightful places. Many people find that playing these number games helps them keep their emotional attachments to several random objects in check by shifting the focus from the item to the counting correlation.

Creating a list is yet another piece of advice that you can use. For other people, starting to clear each space is too much to handle. Perhaps you live in a larger home or have a few smaller spaces that have functioned as general catch-alls and storage. That's alright.

Make a list of every area in your house by sitting down and using it as a tangible representation of your progress. Make a show of crossing a room off when you are through with it. Use a thick Sharpie to scribble over it or write over it. Find a quick and easy method to treat yourself, and then tell everyone how you organized and decluttered that area!

A major first step towards leading a minimalist lifestyle is decluttering your home, and you can also profit from the opportunity to donate many of your belongings to less fortunate people. Think about using this time to allow yourself to experience these memories and meditate on your emotional condition. Then, permit yourself to realize that parting with these things does not mean throwing away your memories. This implies that, just as you could, someone else can now profit from these things and make their priceless memories.

The next item to comprehend is the distinction between a genuine minimalist lifestyle and a commercialized minimalist lifestyle.

Sustaining Minimalism: Some Advice

Being "fully minimalist" is impossible since minimalism is a lifestyle rather than a habit that can be fully formed. You must stick to your minimalist lifestyle to avoid reverting to your flashy and destructive behaviors. These are some pointers to assist you in maintaining your minimalist lifestyle.

Put Your Feelings in Writing

Keep a notebook to record your feelings after converting to a minimalist way of living. Every day, put your feelings in writing and review them. Your encouraging entries in the journal will inspire you to continue these routines.

Please keep a record of any reckless behavior you may have engaged in. Jot down the details and your feelings about it. Next, contrast that with your emotions following a minimalist deed. It will only take a comparison to get you back on track.

Pray

Meditation is the most effective method for enhancing attention and addressing the detrimental processes occurring in your body and mind. Make sure to incorporate it into your everyday routine as it helps you de-stress and reflect on morality. Spending 15 to 20 minutes in meditation can assist you in fully embracing minimalism.

To meditate:

Locate a peaceful area devoid of disturbances and then sit comfortably or lie on the ground.

Choose a comfortable chair if you wish to meditate while seated.

Close your eyes and attempt to breathe as naturally as possible without trying to control it.

Give your entire attention to the movements of your body during each inhalation and exhalation, as well as your breathing. Next, try to observe how your body moves while you breathe. Examine your shoulders, rib cage, tummy, and chest. Make sure you concentrate just on your breathing without attempting to regulate it. Try bringing your attention back to your breathing whenever your thoughts stray. For beginnings, try doing this for four minutes. Once you become used to it, you can continue doing it longer.

Examine how your life compares to others.'

Contrast your new way of living with that of non-minimalists. This is merely to show you how much easier, more convenient, and more laid back your life is compared to those who are used to living extravagant lives; it is not intended to make you feel superior to others or to make you feel inferior. The analogy will encourage you to keep up your minimalist lifestyle.

Use these pointers as support to maintain a minimalist lifestyle.

To Get Well and Succeed

Living a minimalistic lifestyle can make you extremely wealthy, successful, and healthy. You'll be less likely to be tempted to eat unhealthy foods and more inclined to adopt a healthy diet when you can tell what is good and bad.

This will enhance your physical well-being.

Additionally, you stop purchasing and collecting useless items when you concentrate on the things you need and get rid of the rest. You'll start saving more money because you'll start spending less than you make.

Additionally, minimalism supports you in creating meaningful goals and figuring out practical means of achieving them. You start taking your life seriously and chasing your objectives when you focus on the things you need and want rather than those you think you should. You can achieve the success you want when you adopt this mindset.

Henry Ward Beecher once stated that a man's heart is what makes him wealthy. He is wealthy by who he is rather than what he possesses. This statement by Mr. Beecher is well embodied in minimalism; you can purify your heart and spirit by leading a modest lifestyle.

After learning how minimalism enhances your life with beauty, simplicity, and calm, let's discuss how to clear out the various areas of your life and create a meaningful one.

Turning off the TV, phone, and social media when you're not genuinely focusing on anything is another way to help your mind focus on practicing simplicity. It is an encroachment on your existence. You're prevented from success and happiness by the TV sound, the feelings evoked by posts on the Internet, and the disruption of your thoughts every time your phone vibrates with an alert. You do not need to answer to anyone else all the time. Because of this, when it's time to go to bed, turn off all media beforehand to allow your mind to unwind and progressively go to sleep.

You will never be able to declutter with a crowded mind because you will always come up with reasons why you should keep some items and discard others. In actuality, the equation is quite easy. The item in question must be given away if it isn't contributing positively to your life. Give up using grey, black, and all the tones in between. To make things easier when decluttering, start thinking in black and white. Something either improves your life, or it doesn't. No gaps exist between the components. Sure, you might have sentimental items, but only if they hold special importance for you and provide you happiness would you part with them. It's not a practice in deprivation. It is a deliberate exercise in self-control. You have too many things in your life, causing it to become cluttered. But once you've gotten rid of stuff, your house will look bigger, and you'll be happy. Instead of your home being a constant reminder that you still have work to do, you will make it a warm and inviting place to stay.

As a last exercise, shut the door and stand outside the house's main room. Now open the door and act like you have never been in that room. What do you notice right away? It's not like it will be anything purposefully positioned to grab your notice; I'm willing to wager. Rather, it's probably the folded laundry from last night, the leftovers from the kids' schoolwork, the jacket you forgot to hang up yesterday, or anything else that doesn't belong in that room. Organizing your belongings can help you maximize each space in your home. When it's finished, you can enjoy the focus points each space in your house has to offer. That much, I swear to you. Additionally, I guarantee that the simplicity it will bring to your life will make the effort you are about to put in well worth it.

Enhances Your Quality of Life

Health is one of the five characteristics of minimalism—covered in the book's last chapter—. That section's goal is to assist you in concentrating on doing the necessary and appropriate actions for your health while avoiding anything superfluous. Living a minimalist lifestyle aims to help you give up unnecessary material belongings and time-consuming hobbies. Think about the things you do solely to fit in with a group of people or to feel like you have to be like a superhero from a movie or book. Think about all the meals you eat only to look elegant, even when you know deep down that you don't enjoy them. Or consider the foods you consume despite being well aware of their detrimental effects on your health. You can eliminate those things from your life by adopting a minimalist lifestyle. Maintaining a healthy diet is made easier by minimalism. It assists you in getting rid of items that you know are slowly killing you or even things you are unaware are harmful to you. You can live longer and age gracefully with minimalism's support for all of these.

Enhances Your Performance

You have everything it takes to do more meaningful things and accomplish more if you lead a life that isn't rigidly modeled after someone else's, follow your passion, and stop living to appease other people and fit their mold of who you should or shouldn't be. Finally, you can live a life that creates quality physical and psychological space. You benefit from minimalism because it doesn't just eliminate your negative traits. Not at all! It also bestows goodness upon you, substituting virtue for vice and uselessness in your existence.

Assists You In Improving The World

Relationships, development, and contribution are three further aspects of minimalism. All of these are aimed at assisting you in contributing to the betterment of society. As you build genuine relationships with actual people, your authenticity may inspire others to follow suit. You don't take care of yourself poorly. When you adopt a mindset or way of living that enables you to pursue your passion, you may make a greater impact on both the lives of others and your personal development and growth. Being minimalistic does not mean being self-centered. It also means leading a healthy lifestyle, which allows you to treat the environment with kindness and respect, improving the planet.

Aids You Start Feeling Truly Joyful

Based on everything discussed, minimalism is the only path to true happiness—evident to the blind and perhaps audible to the deaf. It will never be an exaggeration to suggest that minimalism is the only path to true pleasure and fulfillment given all the benefits it gives, including the chance to be real and stop living a pretend life, the chance to save more, and the chance to live more and do more and live more. These two can only be attained when we stop pretending to be someone else when we stop caring what other people think of us, when we stop making such an effort to fit our lives into the mold of other people and society, and when we begin to live authentically and not only realize our potential but also assist others in realizing theirs. This is only the case when true happiness is attained—not when we make great efforts to live a false life or fit in, succumbing to the peer pressure of the masses. Living simply is the happy path.

Now that you know the benefits of leading a minimalist lifestyle, it is time to move the conversation to the practical side and explore how to get started.

Chapter 3: First, Decide What

The secret to success is perseverance, and embracing simplicity also requires perseverance. First and foremost, you must be determined to become a true minimalist who never hesitates to refuse free or extra items and fully controls their urges.

How To Strengthen Your Will And Intention

Be inspired to adopt a minimalist lifestyle and become resolute in doing so. You have a better chance of sticking to your intention and accomplishing your goal if you are driven to take action and continue to feed that drive. Our desires to add to and change the things in our lives frequently serve as sources of motivation.

Find out everything you want to change to live a better, cleaner, more peaceful, and more productive existence. This will help you become more determined and intentional about becoming a minimalist. To carry out that:

Get a journal, laptop, or phone, find a quiet place, and consider the reasons behind your pervasive sadness and unease.

Consider asking yourself, "Why am I unhappy?" "What's stopping me?" "Why am I not able to be who I want to be?" How much has consumerism changed my life? Do my temptations make me a victim? If you keep asking yourself these and related questions, you will eventually identify the desire for things you do not want and a lack of worth and meaning in your life as the core causes of your troubles.

Now, close your eyes, list everything you want to be, own, and experience in life, and then picture yourself living it. Put this scenario down on paper in your notebook or laptop.

Now consider everything you need to give up to bring your recently imagined existence to reality. If writing is not your thing, you can even make an audio recording and record whatever you write down in your notebook or Word document.

After reading that list several times, read the life you want to lead a few more times. For you, what is more important? Is clinging to meaningless things more essential to you than manifesting the life of your dreams? Consider the advantages and disadvantages of each, and even though making a choice could take some time, it will probably favor the life you truly want to come true.

For a few weeks, repeat this exercise several times a day or several times per day. It's not necessary to adopt a minimalist lifestyle right away. It must be gradual to ensure that you remain on this journey for the long term and not just a few days. Give yourself enough time to consider your goals and how minimalism may support you in achieving them. You probably want to go ahead rather than backward when you reach that stage.

Once you've decided to live a minimalistic existence, write your intention and make multiple copies of it. To help you recall your intention many times a day, pin it to various locations around your home and your desk at work. This goal will propel you forward and enable you to modify your life as necessary. The next thing you should do is sort everything and declutter your life. A few pointers are useful when decluttering specific rooms or sections in your home.

Not making a purchase.

The radical idea of living better with less is addressed by minimalism. Because material consumption has taken precedence over other values in today's culture, viewing minimalism as a bulwark of austerity is tempting.

Minimalism modifies our interaction with things. We won't be as emotionally invested in them and won't make as many demands, which will cut down on expenditures and purchases. We will steer clear of future consumer chains and put the never-ending question, "Do you know what would be ideal?" out of our minds. Lower upkeep equates to fewer things under our care. That way, the new relationship's goal is not significant cost savings but results from it. Understanding the baselessness of a lavish lifestyle and realizing that expensive things are expensive rather than unique, uncommon, or unusual will lead to financial savings. Conceptually, minimalism does not support zero spending, even when acknowledging this spending drop.

Therefore, cutting back on material purchases does not entail giving up experiences. We'll precisely invest in the things that make us happiest. We're going to the theatre instead of wasting money on trousers. A trip to Asia, rather than a new television. We will tell tales instead of showcasing goods. We'll survive.

Nevertheless, cutting back on purchases sometimes has an unexpected consequence. We might spend more money on something in the same category when something inspires us. Understanding the significance of adding or removing a good from our lives affects our price elasticity. Mathematically speaking, if we buy five shirts instead of ten, we can spend more money on five excellent shirts than ten ordinary ones.

It's not the cult.
Individual and sustained relationships with the world are central to minimalism. It is distinct because each forms a special relationship with things. It is deeply personal because it touches everyone's inner life similarly.
Instead of emphasizing critical thought, many movements—those lacking a solid foundation in their principles—reaffirm themselves by increasing the number of practitioners. Insofar as essentialism and minimalism explore this awareness, and this one-person relationship, critical

thinking—rather than self-justification based on numbers or other external variables—keeps the movement alive.

As we grow more at ease and realize that minimalism is our true state, we will also be more willing to support others in discovering theirs.

Obtaining Assistance

You will reconsider asking for assistance now that you know how difficult it is to say no. It's a positive quality to cultivate, particularly in these modern times, where many individuals honestly discuss their sense of entitlement. However, you should also be aware that you can always rely on others when things are tough.

You can ask your superior or coworkers for aid if you need it with your task. You can hire independent contractors if you're a contractor. If it is insufficient, call a relative, friend, or neighbor. Another choice is to hire experts, particularly if you lack the necessary personnel, equipment, or abilities.

You can avoid more stress by seeking help. You should return the favor in the future, but for now, don't worry too much about it. You can assist if you have the resources—money and time. You can also refuse if you're having trouble.

Time Management

Getting assistance and declining more duties are excellent time-savers. But you can't always count on assistance. Since time is the one resource you cannot acquire, purchase, or store, you must develop good time management skills as a minimalist.

To manage your time effectively, you must first schedule everything. Make time for eight hours of uninterrupted sleep each day. Next, give your morning ritual an hour and a half. Set aside thirty minutes to commute. You have to work for the next three to four hours. After that, take an hour off for lunch and a quick nap. Work for the next few hours. The remainder includes your evening and nighttime routine, meals, and travel home.

You should consider relocating if it takes longer than thirty minutes to get to work. Ask your employer if you can work from home for at least two workdays if you are an employee. Seeking employment elsewhere is an additional choice.

You can set up "time blocks" for your work, morning, and evening routines. Answer calls, messages, and emails about your work during your shift's first ten to fifteen minutes. Take the final five minutes to tidy your desk. Set some time to conduct research as well. Create a tracker for a project and regularly update it with your progress, even if no one asks for a report today. In this manner, you'll always be ready to answer questions about your well-being. Additionally, you'll be conscious of how much work remains.

When it comes to your morning ritual, you should set aside time to get ready, which includes taking a shower, getting dressed, and getting dolled up. You can divide your nightly routine into time blocks for food preparation, cleaning, showering, and going to bed. Time blocks can also be set out for eating breakfast and making your bed.

Time blocking can also be used for domestic tasks. You can set aside a specific day to go grocery shopping every month. Every month, you should set aside one day for general cleaning. You should set up a day for your annual physical and dental examinations. Remember to schedule some downtime for relaxation.

You ought to adhere to the one-minute guideline as well. This implies that you should complete a task in less than a minute. Take a moment to gather worn clothing and place it in the washing basket while you wait for the water to fill the tub or the kettle to boil. Arranging the two pillows on your bed also simply takes a minute. Other quick fixes include clearing the hair from your shower drain cover, emptying your bathroom wastebasket, and organizing your shoe storage. However, try not to complete too many one-minute chores in an hour. Furthermore, if you're working on a crucial activity, disregard the one-minute limit and concentrate solely on it.

With the rise in popularity of minimalism comes the concept of single-tasking. Single-tasking kitchen equipment isn't worth keeping around. Though many encourage multitasking, doing one activity at a time is an underestimated time-saver.

However, multitasking causes attention to be divided. As a result, you become unable to focus, and you generate mediocre work. You might have to do the work again or receive less money. On the other hand, single-tasking makes you more efficient and helps you maintain focus.

At my first corporate job, I worked in a normal Californian office and detested how convoluted everything was. I frequently put in twelve hours a day at work in addition to my eight hours. I once met a coworker who truly amazed me since he would arrive at work at eight and depart at ten or eleven in the morning. This truly astounded me because I had never appeared to be able to leave the office at five o'clock. I used to remain till six or maybe nine o'clock.

I asked this guy, "What's your secret?" one day. What is happening? How come you can depart so early? Firstly, is it even permitted by the company? It appears that the business is unconcerned. Its scheduling is based on outcomes. This means that although your official work schedule is eight to five, you can leave earlier if you can finish your task and get everything out the door sooner. This was the guy who always left at eleven or ten o'clock.

The guy demonstrated how to do it, so I could not express my gratitude. It was a matter of efficiency and process memorization. I was granted permission to depart at midday after adhering strictly to his guidance for several weeks. Until the day I was allowed to leave at ten, I felt that was a major issue. Thus, for a very long time, nobody seemed to mind that this guy and I were departing early. My supervisor didn't care because I completed all my paperwork on time, accurately, and without any mistakes.

If you find it difficult to spend eight hours a day in a glass and concrete cage, find office or corporate work offering results-based scheduling. Put another way, as long as the designated task for the day is completed, they don't care when you leave.

This is a worthwhile substitute for freelance work. You have a great deal of freedom when you freelance. If you work out a deal with the client, you get to decide what needs to be done, how to execute it, and when to turn it in. The nicest thing about all of this is that you can travel a lot and transmit work via the Internet or spend a lot of time with your developing family. Is there anything not to love?

The revenue from freelance work can be highly erratic, which is a disadvantage. There's a lot of money to be made. That isn't the issue. There are months when you can be extremely thin and months when you can be extremely obese.

Working in an office for a company with results-based scheduling is one way to get around this. This gives you the flexibility to quit early and the financial stability of a regular office job.

One further option you have when implementing the concepts of minimalism in your life is to lead a location-neutral lifestyle. This is simply a fancy way of saying you have much mobility. It's not required that you remain in one location.

Did you know that most Americans give up significant economic mobility because of their location-dependent lifestyle? This is according to experts. Put another way, because most Americans prefer to own a home, they pass up these possibilities rather than relocate to areas with the best salaries. A significant amount of opportunity costs result from this.

If you lead an autonomous life, you don't have that issue. Many bloggers travel extensively and earn a respectable living from their travels. Of course, there is a catch to this. Not every person who chooses to blog will earn a five- or even six-figure salary. In actuality, many of them are completely unemployed. I would advise you to go ahead and do so, assuming you are familiar with how the game operates and how to make money regardless of where you are.

Being location-independent allows you to go where the experiences and opportunities are. There is a larger world out there, many more people to meet, issues to work through, and difficulties to overcome, so life is too short to be locked up in a glass and concrete box.

Comprehending TheMindset Of Minimalism

The goal of the minimalist lifestyle is to reduce the amount of worldly stuff you own by removing items from your home, especially those you do not need. There is some truth to this, but minimalism is much more than that.

Less well-known is that minimalism is more about making more room in your life—mind, heart, and soul—for all that is important to you. Being minimalistic involves more than just trying to purge things. The main idea behind minimalism is to eliminate unnecessary items so that only the important things surround you.

Simply put, minimalism is a way of living requiring you to prioritize everything you consider worthwhile and significant. It doesn't demand you give up specific goals or lead a lifestyle. Essentially, minimalism just asks you to be conscious of your true, basic requirements. With this attunement, you may identify what your heart truly desires and follow that instead of listening to conventional wisdom, consumer culture, or stereotypes.

Developing a minimalist attitude can aid in self-awareness and awareness of your requirements. Being self-aware means being conscious of who you are, what you're capable of, and what you want from life.

The minimalist mindset also teaches the idea of letting go of things that do not support your values, beliefs, or principles and replacing them with things you know to enhance your life.

More than just reducing the number of belongings and worldly stuff, minimalism also entails eliminating unhealthy, pointless, unimportant people, ideas, activities, and conventions. If owning an iPhone makes your life better than owning two subpar phones, you should purchase one; if ending a particular relationship makes you feel more alive and free, you should end it.

Living a frugal lifestyle instead of eschewing expensive or luxurious stuff is not the definition of minimalism. It comes down to prioritizing items that enhance your life over anything that lessens its value, whatever you define.

Some minimalists believe that living a travel-inspired, value-driven existence entails packing only two bags and exploring the world in pursuit of the liberating experience of seeing a beautiful sunset.

However, some minimalists believe owning a home is more important than anything else. Therefore, they prioritize building their own house or making adjustments that would enable them to pay off their mortgage more quickly than touring.

In the end, minimalism is all about assisting you in identifying and concentrating on your actual priorities. One of the main tenets of minimalism is being conscious of your requirements.

We frequently find ourselves thinking we desire something, yet we really want something quite different in our hearts. For example, you might need to purchase a car, but in reality, all you need is some downtime and a break from your 16-hour workday.

It can be the hardest portion of the work. Keeping in mind that you are the one who brought everything into your life and house, getting rid of items is not difficult. The hardest thing is getting oneself ready to deal with the idea of letting them go. You have to adopt a minimalist mentality to do this.

5. ACHIEVEMENT OF ONE ROOM AT A TIME

Feeling overwhelmed when cleaning your home is quite simple since you may believe the entire space needs to be decluttered. You could easily become discouraged and begin decluttering due to this feeling. Declutter one room at a time and, if at all possible, divide the space into smaller portions to prevent this. For example, you can divide the bedroom into areas like the closet, dresser, nightstand, bed, etc., if you wish to declutter it. When you declutter the kitchen, you can set up areas for the pantry, cabinets, refrigerator, kitchen counter, drawers, and other items. In this manner, you won't feel pressured to finish everything at once and be more inclined to persevere until the entire house is decluttered.

As you go through each chamber, make three piles on the ground. These will fit into the boxes with labels. After picking up each object, decide which box it belongs in and quickly put it inside it.

Here are some illustrations of decluttering:

Take out your closet: Based on statistical data, we wear about 20% of our wardrobe 80% of the time. This implies that most of us have overstuffed closets full of items we either don't wear or don't fit well anymore. The first step is to go through your closet and throw out everything you rarely or never wear anymore. Do this for thirty days, removing one or two articles of unused clothing daily. You won't miss unused clothing anymore, and your wardrobe will be much more organized.

GET Rid of any décor you don't need: Most of the items we keep in our houses serve no purpose. They were either on sale the day we walked into the store. Regretfully, they detract from the house accents that tell your unique story and emphasize your values for you and your visitors. Examine the house with an astute and perceptive gaze. Remove most ornaments, leaving only the most exquisite and meaningful ones.

GET Rid of any toys your kids aren't playing with: Too frequently; we err on the side of "more is better,", especially regarding our children. Most Americans buy far more toys than their children will ever need. And as a result, our children don't think they need to develop their creative or improvising skills. Remove most of the toys and save the ones your children play with. But before you do this, it will be wise to speak with your kids.

Eliminate the excessive number of television sets you own: Every day, the average American watches TV for four and a half hours. The average American home has 2.73 TV sets compared to 2.55 persons, which is more TVs than people. The average American home has a TV on for eight hours and fifteen minutes a day—more than one-third of the day—which means we essentially settle down on the couch and watch TV while life slowly goes by. Try living with fewer TVs by selling or donating most of them and spending money on one high-quality TV. As a result, you will watch less; when you do, you'll probably watch with the family, strengthening your relationship.

DISCARD THE DUPLICATE: Don't forget to discard duplicates when tidying each room. Place the second measuring cup in a box if you have any. Pack it in a box if you have several copies of the same book or magazine edition. After filling your box, label it "duplicates" and store it hidden for 30 days. Donate the box if you don't need anything in it or if you forget everything you placed in it.

Make room for everything: Find a home for anything you intend to keep. Because there isn't a single location where everything can be kept, ensuring each item has a specific area to be maintained helps prevent things from ending up everywhere. Since everyone knows to put things back where they belong after usage, this will also stop clutter from building up.

Destructive and vacuum room: Not many things can revitalize a space, like cleaning. Examine the neat space, which you might not have had the opportunity to see in months or perhaps years. Clear any dirt and debris from objects and surfaces; remove any cobwebs and repaint if you feel it is needed. In this manner, the space becomes tidy and comfortable. Staying in becomes a genuine pleasure.

For Elderly Kids

Taking an older child shopping can be rather challenging when they want everything. Even with a big budget, it might get old quickly. Refusing to give anything to them is the simplest approach to show kids that they cannot have everything. This is one of those things that is easier said than done.

But from the moment you create your list, inform them that you will only buy what is on it and follow through. Allowing children to assist you in creating the list is one way to involve them. As you compile your list, educate them on the distinction between needs and wants.

Ask them to check the refrigerator, for instance, and tell them what you are missing. While cookies are a wish, milk is a must. Just buy the items on the list when you visit the store. Don't get anything if it's not on the list, even if you need it. Ask them if it's on the list when they make a request. Inform them no if they respond negatively. They will eventually realize we don't need it, at which point we won't purchase it.

Go out of the store, as for those meltdowns. Go to your car after leaving your full basket where it is. They go home after continuing to act out.

Once they settle down, go back to shopping. When you go home, and they're not eating what they requested, tell them you were unable to complete your shopping because they wouldn't cooperate.

They'll quickly realize that going shopping is essential. It requires endurance and patience. They will eventually come to comprehend.

For Young Adults and Teens

It might be hard for a child to know what they truly need and want when they have grown up with everything they could want bought for them. Consider providing them an allowance, and let them know that while you take care of the necessities, they will be responsible for getting anything else.

They will come to understand what they truly need and desire. They will learn not to waste anything from it. Additionally, it will get them ready to take on independent duties.

Teens who work should be given some responsibility as soon as they start working. They ought to be able to cover the cost of petrol if they are driving. They ought to assist with insurance. If they're working, that is.

I know of one mom who had to teach her child the hard way how costly petrol may get. She was frequently asked to take her pals around because she was the only one among them who could drive. She was begging for more money for petrol all the time.

Her parents initially believed that she had to do it to get to school. It was just too pricey after a time. So, her folks would take her car every Sunday night and fill it up. That was it till Sunday the following week when the petrol ran out. It would have to be the bus for her. The daughter would run out of petrol, so she first used the bus two or three days a week.

She ran out of petrol multiple times, forcing her to spend the weekends at home. She eventually figured out how to get her buddies to pitch in for gas. She stopped using the bus in a short amount of time. Sometimes, it's necessary to learn a lesson the hard way.

Internal, Not External, Is Minimalism.

We lay out seven guiding principles in our first book, Simplify, to assist anyone in decluttering their life and home. By clearing out a large portion of the material clutter from their homes, countless people have found freedom thanks to the book's guiding ideas. The exterior aspects of existence are the focus of the book nearly entirely. Furthermore, although it aids in releasing individuals from the congestion outside of themselves, it stops short of assisting them in achieving inner freedom and harmony.

I've discovered that simplicity is always an internal decision. Once the surface clutter is cleared, minimalism can tackle the most fundamental emotional problems that affect our relationships and overall well-being.

MINIMALISM IS ENTIRELY IMPOSSIBLE.

Living a minimalist lifestyle is doable. My family is a real example of this. We were just an ordinary suburban family of four, storing as many things as our credit cards and income would allow. Then, minimalism was discovered. We have consciously decided to live frugally and will never return to our previous way of living. And we are living examples of how everybody who aspires to minimalism can do it in a unique and achievable way.

The people who take the time to ask follow-up questions and are generally curious about "what minimalism is anyway" are usually drawn to the lifestyle's tenets. It provides nearly what our hearts have been aching for all along.

The Advantages of a Minimalist Lifestyle

Make space for the essentials.

We make room and calm when cleaning our closets and rubbish drawers. We no longer feel constricted and can breathe normally. Make space in our lives for meaningful things rather than goods.

2. Greater liberty

The accumulation of possessions ties us down like an anchor. We always worry that we will lose everything we own. If you let it go, you'll feel freedom from greed, debt, preoccupation, and overworking that you've never felt before.

g. The Advantages of Simplicity

Of course, there are advantages to everything.

The following are the top eight advantages of living a minimalist lifestyle:

1 - Making and Value the Essential Things in Life.

Once everything that you no longer require in your life or your home has been removed from it, you experience more room and tranquility—not just in your surroundings but also within yourself. You begin to feel like you can breathe again and will have more space to occupy the things you truly enjoy.

2. The necessary freedom

You might not realize it, but the things you've accumulated over the years can weigh you down and give you a certain amount of stress you can release. People are sometimes "terrified" to throw away their belongings but trust me, once you let go of the things you no longer need. You will undoubtedly feel a liberation unlike anything you have ever experienced, free from preoccupation, debt, greed, and overworking.

3- Put your interests and well-being first.

Most people are unaware of how they are using their time. Usually, people use the excuse that they don't have enough time to do what they want to do. However, they fail to realize that instead of using that time to do what they love, they are wasting it on activities they normally don't want to do.

4-Material possessions don't matter

Everything in our immediate environment is just a diversion from what normally exists inside us. Happiness cannot be purchased with money, but comfort may be.

Individuals are always falling victim to the materialism trap. Therefore, try to remind yourself of the delusion of happiness you might be living when you see anything in the media you believe you need.

Acknowledge the items that, while enjoyable, you may not require.

5-Calm Mind

Stress is released when material possessions are let rid of. However, the instant you clutch on these objects, tension is generated due to your fear of losing them. You can finally feel tranquil and at ease once you have decluttered your life and let go of any attachments to these things.

You have less to worry about the less stuff you own.

6-Emotional Well-Being

It is obvious that when you simplify your life, the things that matter to you will gravitate toward you, leading to bliss.

Being more efficient will also enable you to find greater happiness. You can enjoy and value yourself if you can refocus on your priorities.

7-Refuse to Give Up

When you consider it, Buddhist monks typically don't experience anxiety since they have nothing to lose. Once your fear of material stuff is gone, pursuing your areas of excellence is advisable.

8. Self-assurance

A minimalist lifestyle encourages uniqueness and independence, which ultimately leads to confidence.

Here are a few easy morning rituals that can set the tone and course for your day.

1. Spending the first ninety minutes of the morning in meditation. Ten minutes

of guided meditation will help you reset and get ready to take on the day. You can eliminate all of your worries by practicing meditation. The breathing component of meditation, in particular, helps your brain absorb a lot of new oxygen, allowing you to concentrate clearly and be productive in the morning.

2. A glass of warm water squeezed with a fresh lemon. This aids in stabilizing your stomach's alkaline pH. Also, your body will get hydrated by the warm water. When you drink this after going without food or liquids for six to seven hours while you sleep, your body gets restocked with the fluids it needs to stay healthy and productive during the day.

3. An Americano-style hot cup of black coffee. Coffee use has many health advantages. As a naturally occurring psychotic medication, caffeine is taken by millions of individuals worldwide. Coffee, which has Arabic roots but was made popular by Europeans, increases focus and encourages productivity. When coffee is drunk while fasting, it helps mobilize fat and boosts immunity. Coffee aids in the treatment of depression. Having a cup of coffee in the morning can help you stay optimistic and in a good mood throughout the day.

4. A modest breakfast. Because eating a lot of carbohydrates releases hormones that promote sleep, eating a large meal in the morning will make you feel

drowsy. I suggest eating a low-fat, high-protein breakfast, such as egg whites, with a few slices of whole wheat bread and fresh fruit. That is all. Remain straightforward and understated. A light breakfast will enable you to focus clearly and be more productive throughout the workday.

Physical Setup

Having psychologically prepared yourself to let go may make it easier to go out and physically get the equipment you'll need to clean up your house.

If at all possible, limit your purchases to the following products:

Sacks for trash

Bags for recycling (to distinguish from the trash)

Select between rubber or latex gloves.

Zip-ties

Supplies for cleaning (only if you don't already have any)

These necessities will facilitate your cleanup efforts and make it simpler for you to get rid of big mounds of stuff.

It is imperative that, unless you think it is required, you do not purchase anything more than what is on the list above. Recall that your goal is to reduce your possessions, not acquire new ones. Ask someone to do it for you if you do not yet trust yourself to avoid buying unnecessary items. However, this will only work as a short-term fix since you will eventually have to take care of yourself and learn to resist the need to acquire unnecessary items.

On this journey to self-improvement, one of the hardest things you will do is prepare yourself, especially mentally and even physically (fighting the need to not overbuy). But after it's done, your work will be less stressful and more labor-intensive. Thank you for finishing this step if you have! Next, We will examine the objects in your house to determine how to arrange them and start the actual disposal procedure. Don't give up yet; you've done incredibly well so far. Proceed!

Putting The Organisation Process In Motion

Organizing your life and belongings with categories is the first step towards starting the sorting process. This is when the real physical decluttering of your home will start.

Depending on the amount and variety of items you have hoarded over the years, you might require more categories than less. You've mentally prepared yourself to go through this process, but you will still be unsure about what to keep and throw away. Organizing your belongings into categories will make it easier to give them value and show you how many identical or almost identical goods you have.

First, make a physical location in your house to arrange your belongings according to categories. Don't make a category just for wrappers or any form of packaging. Alternatively, to be more precise, just mark that stuff as garbage if it can't be recycled and recycle if it can. You will also establish other categories, such as those for paper, plastic, toys, hazardous garbage, non-functioning gadgets, clothes, books, wearable shoes, and so on, and for donations of clothing and other items.

While asking friends or relatives for assistance can be awkward, it will expedite the process and keep you from being tempted to hold onto items that should be removed. This process can be time-consuming. If you are struggling to start letting go and have someone or a group of people supporting you, you can run an exercise where each participant chooses five things to throw away. You are unable to override their choice or engage in debate with them. You have to give in if they say it's garbage or has to go. This is undoubtedly the tough-love method, but it can give you a head start on your recovery.

The next stage is to create space to arrange even more after dividing everything into groups. This entails starting with the apparent things you take out of your house. As previously stated, all packaging and wrappers are garbage (or recyclables), so they must be handled as such. Furthermore, any newspapers, journals, fliers, etc., that you have previously perused or that contain a date other than this week are recyclables. If you don't already have one, get a car, load everything in it, and drive to your area's recycling and rubbish disposal facilities. Avoid leaving stuff outside your house for collection, as you could be tempted to go back and retrieve everything.

Advantages for the Environment

Leading a minimalist lifestyle is indeed better for the environment. You may utilize fewer natural resources on the earth by consuming less, polluting less, and consuming fewer goods overall. For a considerable amount of time, the world has been concerned about the depletion of the planet's natural resources and other environmental issues like air and water pollution, wildlife conservation, and climate change. A minimalist lifestyle can help the environment and other associated energy-saving concerns. Can you picture the effect of a sizable portion of the global population choosing to lead this kind of lifestyle? Even better, what if everyone took part in it?

A Clear and Concentrated Thought

The clearing of the mind is another advantage of this way of living. It purges the unnecessary items from your life and does the same to your ideas. This is crucial because the state of the mind on the inside determines everything in the outside world. Once you can calm your thoughts, a lot of mental clutter and the effects of unsupportive and negative people can be released from your mind. You can then recognize and differentiate between life's ambitions and unwanted goals. You may see your goals and desires more clearly and with clarity once the clutter in your head has been removed. Consequently, sharpening your attention on your actual objectives and developing the motivation to achieve them.

When grit and perseverance permeate your mind and cause you to lose motivation for success, your life's interests become more apparent. You'll then be able to comprehend your goals and effectively put together the methods and essential actions required to achieve them if you have a clear mind and are focused. As a result, this fourth benefit causes pleasure to increase because it frees up more time for you to engage in enabling and more productive activities.

Better Living Area

Of course, having a clean mind comes second to having a tidy home. The main tenet of a minimalist lifestyle is having less. Therefore, your house and place of employment should be clutter-free or have less in them. A home is a private, holy space that offers safety, comfort, and opportunities for introspection and contemplation. While you might not be able to control your surroundings when you're not at home, you have complete control over where you live. You can establish a peaceful space where you can concentrate and center your thoughts on the more essential things by simply holding onto the few items that have personal significance or positive effects on you.

Most importantly, having extra room where you spend most of your time can improve your mental and emotional health. After a long day at work, an event, or a night out with loved ones, returning home to a calm setting may be quite beneficial for relieving tension and other built-up stress. A clean environment improves happiness and concentration, so the unimportant things won't matter.

But putting the past behind you goes hand in hand with organizing and downsizing. It's bidding farewell to items you formerly utilized and required. Once you have let go of the past and made space for the present, your soul will feel relieved. We are liberated from all previous responsibilities by simplicity. Everything has a function. We should gladly give up the item as soon as its intended use is accomplished to create space for new things, including memories. You see, maintaining proper housekeeping is a journey of self-improvement.

The idea is to determine what should be given away and what should be kept because it is not necessary or significant.

We always refer to an annual cycle whenever we use the word frequently. We regain our ability to perceive what we like and seek with the aid of this selection process, and we begin to focus more intently on the things we enjoy right now. Living in an environment that has been meticulously cleaned up, freed from the past, and filled with items that one likes and uses frequently in the here and now gives rise to this incredibly powerful feeling of joy.

When you read the last few sentences, did you notice anything? Everything is connected to your mental order (look at your mind map). This includes ideas you've had but never followed through on or implemented, desires you've never set goals for, started but abandoned projects, long-lost colleagues, bills you've never paid off, and courses you've started but haven't found fulfilling. Numerous such instances exist. Minimalism examines both the inside and outside and applies its filter to everything. All that's left is always what we love, what we need, what brings us joy, and what concerns us right now.

Disarray

The disorder results when things and ideas that are neither needed nor cherished are held upon and don't have specific locations. Therefore, disorder always affects physical things (clothing, books, knick-knacks, etc.) and nonphysical things (ideas, wants, etc.).

The main causes of the disorder are overwork and chronic laziness. One is aware that the jacket needs to be hung up after work rather than flung over the couch. However, when one is overburdened, they tend to put things off. Thus, one must consent to alter conduct and break old patterns to live in order. It always begins in the mind. You need to start paying attention to these things.

It is the most powerful weapon against chaos to practice minimalism. As previously said, you just have to cope with a small number of possessions; thus, clutter is easier to prevent. All you have to do is consent to step outside your comfort zone once and use the minimalism filter to help you fight your mess. After that, all that is left is to use the appropriate system to automate and consolidate the new way of living.

I frequently see clients who appear to lead organized lives. However, appearances can frequently be deceiving. Since the problem is not addressed from the root, even apparent order is inherently chaotic and stressful. If you haven't dealt with every item, keeping anything in the basement or boxes under your bed doesn't make sense.

To take a step toward minimalism, you must determine the worth of every single object, including digital documents, clothes, linens, extra cables, spoons, and so on. Ultimately, minimalism allows you to identify each item on your list and its location in storage. If you cannot accomplish this, you still possess too many items or have not given each object your full attention.

Diminish fear

Inhale. Even though these are difficult and complex times, minimalism can help you regain control. The clutter around you merely worsens everything, making you anxious by organizing your surroundings and home. One of the most important aspects of anxiety is hypervigilance, which makes you extremely alert to every person, thing, circumstance, and possible scenario. It can be draining and tiresome. However, as you set out on your minimalist adventure, you'll discover that your perspective starts to shift. Letting go of things and the bad feelings associated with them or oneself can be accomplished. You can start to let go of something and recognize it for what it is—or maybe no longer is—when you consciously toss it away.

Similarly, intentionality prevents you from becoming overwhelmed by your environment by making you concentrate on just one item at a time. When the decluttering process is over, having space will help you focus on other areas of your life that you might have overlooked because you were preoccupied with worry and clutter. You give yourself permission to succeed and unwind by setting up a space where you feel at ease, prepared, and focused.

aids in concentration

We will be working with minimalism here, so it will help you focus on all the important things in your life, not just the jobs you have to finish. It will also assist you in focusing on your goals. You're not always thinking about the mess around you; therefore, you have more time. Decluttering just gives you room to unwind, which helps you focus, similar to how it reduces anxiety.

It can easily make you feel like a failure, which can trigger anxiety and sadness. Clutter diverts your attention and makes you feel you must multitask when you shouldn't. Organizing a workspace or a kitchen can improve your experience by encouraging more organized and effective task completion. You will still be able to focus, but staying focused for longer stretches of time will be simpler, which will increase your productivity.

Boost output

The efficiency with which one completes duties is referred to as productivity. Like in the previous scenario, clutter has made it difficult for you to concentrate, so you were unable to do the assignment. It has a snowball effect since being behind schedule makes concentrating harder, which lowers output.

You can walk to your desk, pull out your laptop and charger, and get to work fairly instantly if you clear out a mostly clutter-free space. You don't have to wipe up coffee stains and bring dirty mugs to the kitchen, nor do you have to sift through mountains of books and papers. You can completely and unhinderedly concentrate on the task without being distracted or influenced by your environment. Making a place where you can think about things other than the objects in the room is guaranteed by minimalism. Items have a function, and you can no longer utilize them when they hinder you from achieving your objective or fail to fulfill it.

A 3-Step Guide to Help You Transition Into a Minimalist Lifestyle

Being a minimalist requires changing your perspective on goods and other ownership issues. Therefore, it's not an easy journey. But being difficult does not always mean that something is unachievable. You may ease yourself into minimalism in several ways besides adhering to the one straightforward rule: rid your life of anything you don't need and hold onto what you value.

This portion of the book goes over the several steps you should take to become a minimalist as simply as possible:

Establish A Precise Intention, Deadline, And Goal.

Since minimalism is individualized and means different things to different people, it is obvious that you first need to identify what minimalism means to you and what a minimal life looks like. For you, what does it mean? You must respond to that query first.

Does minimalism entail, to you, merely having the necessities in life? Does it entail removing items from your thoughts and space that you haven't worked on, viewed, or utilized in months? Does this imply that you have to sell the things you don't need, stop acquiring new goods, and then purchase high-quality versions of the things you need? As you can see, there are various variations of minimalism. For this reason, defining what it means to you and making a firm purpose for living such a life are the first steps towards incorporating it into your life.

Since minimalism is about simplifying your life, your objective should be to live it with the things that bring you joy, passion, and life—with what you actually need. Once you have established what this means for you, begin to eliminate anything—mental, physical, or otherwise—that does not contribute to the life you and your loved ones want to lead. The core of minimalism is getting rid of everything that prevents you from achieving and doing more of the things you truly desire out of life.

To do this:

Make a list of everything you need to accomplish to begin living the life you have clearly defined for yourself (visualize it vividly).

Make a strategy outlining how you aim to declutter your home, mind, and other spaces if your definition of minimalism requires you.

Ensure the plan is clear and each phase is as simple as possible.

Write down your aspirations for minimalism and explain why they are significant to you and how they will enable you to have a simple but fulfilling life.

Once your goals are established, set a timeframe to reach your objectives. For example, assign a deadline to your to-do list, bedroom, lounge area, and closet decluttering tasks. You have to take immediate action because of a deadline.

What Is Minimalism, Chapter 1? It Doesn't Mean Living On The Least Possible...

You've likely heard "minimalism," but what does it mean? Most critics think being minimalist only means giving up life's joys, moving into a forest, constructing an entirely natural home, and emerging as the "new Gandhi." While some minimalists DO aspire to live that way, that isn't the main goal.

Eliminating unnecessary items gathered in your life over time is the fundamental component of minimalism. Emphasizing that minimalism is more than just getting rid of material belongings is crucial, even though it's a good place to start! It is a broad method of living that encompasses all facets of your existence. Put another way, it's about clearing out the unnecessary things from your life to make place for the things that matter to you. This means sorting through your belongings to see what matters to you and what doesn't, then getting rid of the latter.

As obvious as it may seem, the reality is that far too frequently, we become so engrossed in our hectic lives that we lose sight of the distinction between what we genuinely want out of life and what we believe we SHOULD want (based on the social order, the surroundings, or our views).

Ultimately, this leads to a loss of value. We acquire MORE "things," surround ourselves with MORE people, and take on MORE tasks to fill that hole. On the other hand, minimalism encourages us to make conscious decisions again, which helps us live intentionally.

Everyone's definition of minimalism is undoubtedly unique. Each of us has certain things that are particular to us.

Let's imagine you encounter a group of approximately fifty people explaining to you what minimalism means to them.

You'll come up with at least fifty distinct interpretations of minimalism. That's the beauty of minimalism: as long as you prioritize what matters most, you can determine how much of it is appropriate for you.

So, what are the advantages of embracing minimalism? The following advantages of minimalism may provide you with the inspiration you need to adopt the way of life:

Mind Clarity

There is no denying the link between our emotional and mental well-being and the things we own. Do you recall the Saturday you spent organizing the items in your spare bedroom or storage unit for the whole day? After you completed it, how did you feel? Probably relieved? You likely thought about those things all week, so getting rid of them helped you relax.

Imagine feeling that way every single minute of the day. One advantage of simplicity is that.

Increased Liberty

To please people we don't like, financial counselors say the harsh reality is that "we buy things we don't need with money we don't have."

You'll be shocked to learn how many material possessions you either already own, wish to acquire, or have worked hard to obtain—that you don't even want—if you give it some serious thought.

You can release this strain and do what YOU want by adopting a minimalist lifestyle. You will, therefore, be able to work for yourself, travel, take a sabbatical, and even secure a position that truly fulfills you.

www.ingramcontent.com/pod-product-compliance
Lightning Source LLC
Chambersburg PA
CBHW052144110526
44591CB00012B/1856